NATHANIEL J HALL

Nathaniel J Hall is an award-winning playwright, actor, filmmaker and HIV activist from Manchester. He writes, directs, inspires and produces bold and provocative, socially-minded work. He studied Theatre and Performance at the University of Leeds (Bretton Hall) graduating with First Class Honours in 2008.

A leading voice in the fight against HIV stigma, his community-led creative activism tackling HIV stigma and shame has reached hundreds of thousands through creative workshops and talks, and tens of millions through broadcast media and print.

An expert by experience in the art of telling autobiographical stories to improve health and wellbeing, Nathaniel creates theatre and films with (and for) historically marginalised people and communities and has delivered projects for Contact Theatre, The Royal Exchange Theatre, 20 Stories High, Wellcome, Manchester Pride, George House Trust and Manchester University NHS Foundation Trust.

Living with HIV since the age of sixteen, Nathaniel has used his personal story as a vehicle to educate, destigmatise and empower others to live boldly and with pride. Now a prominent voice in HIV and LGBTQ+ activism he is regularly invited to speak on the subject by the media.

As a television actor, Nathaniel appears in *It's A Sin* – the Channel 4 drama about HIV/AIDS in 1980s Britain by Russell T Davies. Nathaniel recently fronted a Channel 4 documentary on the HIV subculture of bug chasing.

He is Co-Artistic Director of Dibby Theatre, lives in Salford with his partner Seán, and is dad to two dogs – Peggy and Fred.

www.nathanieljhall.co.uk
@nathanieljhall

Other Titles in this Series

Annie Baker
THE ANTIPODES
THE FLICK
INFINITE LIFE
JOHN

Mike Bartlett
THE 47TH
ALBION
BULL
GAME
AN INTERVENTION
KING CHARLES III
MIKE BARTLETT PLAYS: TWO
MRS DELGADO
SCANDALTOWN
SNOWFLAKE
UNICORN
VASSA *after* Gorky
WILD

Jez Butterworth
THE FERRYMAN
THE HILLS OF CALIFORNIA
JERUSALEM
JEZ BUTTERWORTH PLAYS: ONE
JEZ BUTTERWORTH PLAYS: TWO
MOJO
THE NIGHT HERON
PARLOUR SONG
THE RIVER
THE WINTERLING

Jessie Cave
SUNRISE

Mohamed-Zain Dada
BLUE MIST
DIZZY

JJ Green
A-TYPICAL RAINBOW

Nathaniel J Hall
FIRST TIME

Rose Heiney
ELEPHANTS
ORIGINAL DEATH RABBIT

Lucy Kirkwood
BEAUTY AND THE BEAST
  with Katie Mitchell
BLOODY WIMMIN
THE CHILDREN
CHIMERICA
HEDDA *after* Ibsen
THE HUMAN BODY
IT FELT EMPTY WHEN THE HEART
  WENT AT FIRST BUT IT IS
  ALRIGHT NOW
LUCY KIRKWOOD PLAYS: ONE
MOSQUITOES
NSFW
RAPTURE
TINDERBOX
THE WELKIN

Larry Kramer
THE NORMAL HEART

Haley McGee
AGE IS A FEELING

Tommy Murphy
HOLDING THE MAN *after* Timothy Conigrave
STRANGERS IN BETWEEN

Sam Steiner
KANYE THE FIRST
LEMONS LEMONS LEMONS LEMONS
  LEMONS
A TABLE TENNIS PLAY
YOU STUPID DARKNESS!

Jack Thorne
2ND MAY 1997
AFTER LIFE *after* Hirokazu Kore-eda
BUNNY
BURYING YOUR BROTHER IN
  THE PAVEMENT
A CHRISTMAS CAROL *after* Dickens
THE END OF HISTORY…
HOPE
JACK THORNE PLAYS: ONE
JACK THORNE PLAYS: TWO
JUNKYARD
LET THE RIGHT ONE IN
  after John Ajvide Lindqvist
THE MOTIVE AND THE CUE
MYDIDAE
THE SOLID LIFE OF SUGAR WATER
STACY & FANNY AND FAGGOT
WHEN WINSTON WENT TO WAR WITH
  THE WIRELESS
WHEN YOU CURE ME
WOYZECK *after* Büchner

debbie tucker green
BORN BAD
DEBBIE TUCKER GREEN PLAYS: ONE
DIRTY BUTTERFLY
EAR FOR EYE
HANG
NUT
A PROFOUNDLY AFFECTIONATE,
  PASSIONATE DEVOTION TO SOMEONE
  (– NOUN)
RANDOM
STONING MARY
TRADE & GENERATIONS
TRUTH AND RECONCILIATION

Phoebe Waller-Bridge
FLEABAG

Tom Wells
BIG BIG SKY
BROKEN BISCUITS
DRIP *with* Matthew Robins
FOLK
JUMPERS FOR GOALPOSTS
THE KITCHEN SINK
ME, AS A PENGUIN
STUFF

Nathaniel J Hall

TOXIC

NICK HERN BOOKS
London
www.nickhernbooks.co.uk

A Nick Hern Book

Toxic first published in Great Britain as a paperback original in 2025
by Nick Hern Books Limited, The Glasshouse, 49a Goldhawk Road, London
W12 8QP

Toxic copyright © 2025 Nathaniel J Hall

Nathaniel J Hall has asserted his right to be identified as the author of this work

Cover photography by Lee Baxter, back cover photography by Dawn Kilner

Designed and typeset by Nick Hern Books, London
Printed in Great Britain by Mimeo Ltd, Huntingdon, Cambridgeshire PE29 6XX

A CIP catalogue record for this book is available from the British Library

ISBN 978 1 83904 442 7

CAUTION All rights whatsoever in this play are strictly reserved. Requests to reproduce the text in whole or in part should be addressed to the publisher.

Amateur Performing Rights Applications for performance, including readings and excerpts, by amateurs in the English language throughout the world should be addressed to the Performing Rights Department, Nick Hern Books, The Glasshouse, 49a Goldhawk Road, London W12 8QP, *tel* +44 (0)20 8749 4953, *email* rights@nickhernbooks.co.uk, except as follows:

Australia: ORiGiN Theatrical, Level 1, 213 Clarence Street, Sydney NSW 2000, tel +61 (2) 8514 5201, *email* enquiries@originmusic.com.au, *web* www.origintheatrical.com.au

New Zealand: Play Bureau, 20 Rua Street, Mangapapa, Gisborne, 4010, *tel* +64 21 258 3998, *email* info@playbureau.com

Professional Performing Rights Applications for performance by professionals in any medium and in any language throughout the world (including by amateur stock companies in the USA and Canada) should be addressed in the first instance to Nick Hern Books

No performance of any kind may be given unless a licence has been obtained. Applications should be made before rehearsals begin. Publication of this play does not necessarily indicate its availability for amateur performance.

www.nickhernbooks.co.uk/environmental-policy

Nick Hern Books' authorised representative in the EU is
Easy Access System Europe – Mustamäe tee 50, 10621 Tallinn, Estonia
email gpsr.requests@easproject.com

Introduction
Nathaniel J Hall

In 2017, after nearly fifteen years of living in secrecy and shame as HIV-positive (diagnosed at sixteen, after my first sexual encounter – talk about unlucky), I decided to break my silence. I wrote an emotional letter to my family, and then did what felt completely natural to me, a professional show-off, but a move that would horrify most other normal people: I turned my story into a one-person play called *First Time*.

Commissioned by Waterside Arts in South Manchester, I figured it would help me unload some of my emotional baggage and maybe give my sinking acting career a boost. If not, well, I'd wave my white flag with the sinking ship and slump off quietly to find a new career.

Much to my surprise, however, *First Time* struck a chord with people – big time. Buzzfeed News picked up the story, then BBC News, MTV, Radio 5 Live… I was even invited to the BBC Breakfast couch to chat with Charlie and Naga. A few weeks earlier, I'd only just told my parents about my HIV status. Now, I was trending higher than Jennifer Aniston's bangs (I kid you not). Talk about zero to a hundred in just a few weeks.

Over the next four years, *First Time* was performed over a hundred times, including an award-winning run at the Edinburgh Festival Fringe, receiving both critical acclaim and audience admiration. It also sparked a powerful wave of HIV disclosures, with one person sharing they had lived in silence for thirty years before coming out publicly at a post-show discussion. These stories inspired me to create *In Equal Parts*, a community-led outreach project tackling HIV stigma and shame. To date the project has reached over seventy thousand people and continues to empower others with HIV to live boldly and without shame.

It wasn't all down to me, of course. *First Time* rode the wave of a shift in confidence among people living with HIV, driven by scientific breakthroughs and the work of activists and charities. In the UK, a landmark High Court ruling expanded access to PrEP* across the country, and this, along with the recently penned 'Undetectable = Untransmittable' (U=U)** message, was helping to shift public attitudes and reduce stigma.

The success of *First Time* kept that impending career change at bay. I landed a role in *It's A Sin*, Russell T Davies' hit Channel 4 drama, and as the only openly HIV-positive actor in the cast, another whirlwind media frenzy ensued – one so big it required a spreadsheet to manage. (Shoutout to my partner Seán for being a total freak in the [spread] sheets.)

But despite all this public success, my personal life was still a mess. Drugs, risky and compulsive sex, alcohol – they were still plaguing my world. In 2019, I found myself trying to escape a deeply problematic, co-dependent and, at times, abusive relationship. And looking around at my community, I knew I wasn't alone.

Many of my LGBTQ+ friends were stuck in similar toxic cycles of substance misuse, unhealthy relationships and risky sex. I dove into books like *Straight Jacket* by Matthew Todd and *We Can Do Better Than This* compiled by Amelia Abraham, cried my eyes out, and eventually started therapy – where I cried a whole swimming pool.

I began to realise that I'd been using alcohol, drugs and sex to mask the emotional pain caused by a world that had treated me badly, and when my own compounded trauma collided with someone else's, well, it was a car crash waiting to happen.

Through creative workshops and research, I learned that many LGBTQ+ people – particularly those at the intersections of disability, race and gender non-conformity – carry additional layers of trauma. This discovery broke my heart, and I cried an ocean. I was left asking, *'when the world treats us so horribly, why do we end up treating ourselves and each other so badly too?'*

First Time had helped me reconcile the trauma of my early HIV diagnosis at sixteen, but now I felt like I'd sold a bit of a lie. Everything in the play *was* true (except for the holiday disco, which was actually karaoke – nobody wants to hear me screeching a rendition of 'My Heart Will Go On' night after night), but something didn't feel quite right.

First Time was crafted as a 'queer rags-to-riches' story that often brought audiences to their feet in ovation. But there were no standing ovations in my personal life. After the high of the Edinburgh Fringe run, I had to leave my last relationship for my safety, sell all my possessions in a week, and move back in with my parents. Real life felt like a one-star review, not the five-star triumph I had portrayed on stage.

Then the global pandemic hit. Amid the chaos of those months, I had time to reflect on everything. I knew I needed to face my pain head-on – just like I had with *First Time*. That's when *Toxic* was born.

Unlike *First Time*, *Toxic* is only semi-autobiographical. It weaves in stories from other LGBTQ+ people I met through workshops, touching on other issues including racism, class, sexuality and gender. As I wrote, I realised how deeply historical marginalisation and societal prejudice continue to affect queer relationships. *Toxic* explores how these 'minority stressors' show up in our intimate lives, often with devastating consequences.

Through the play, I also wanted to represent a broader spectrum of experiences. As a white writer, I was nervous about portraying a person of colour in a play about an abusive relationship, but the stories I heard from queer people of colour spoke so much truth to power that I couldn't ignore them. At community script-sharing events for LGBTQ+ people of colour and their partners, early drafts were met with critique, especially around racial stereotypes I had stumbled into. I listened, leaned into the discomfort, and worked hard to do better. I'm forever grateful to those who helped me – particularly Susan Kerr – who challenged me with kindness and compassion.

Writing *Toxic* has been a deep, humbling lesson in unlearning, especially when it comes to racism. Tackling systemic inequality requires tough, uncomfortable conversations, and I've learned that dismantling these structures is the work of all of us – white, Black, brown, and every shade in between.

Toxic doesn't end with a standing ovation like *First Time*. It's not that it's not good – I'll let you be the judge of that. It's just that it dares to sit with the messiness and complexity of life. It still has heart, hope and humour (I try to write serious drama, but everyone seems to laugh, and maybe that's a good thing). In a way, *Toxic* is a love letter to all my exes and to myself, an apology for how things turned out, but also a thank-you for the life lessons learnt.

Ultimately, *Toxic* is a story of queer survival and resilience in the face of relentless societal prejudice and shame. I hope that when people read or watch the play, they laugh with us, cry with us, and, most importantly, reach deep inside themselves and say to their own wounded inner child, *'I've got you, we're going to be okay, we'll survive this, together.'*

* Medication taken pre-emptively before sex that is highly effective at stopping transmission.

** Research that proved people with HIV on effective mediation with an undetectable viral load can't pass the virus on.

Foreword
Susan Kerr

As a little Black girl, the brutality of the world terrified me, and I found myself desperate to understand why. I hoped that if I could grasp the root of hatred, I could somehow protect myself. This obsession with understanding became a passion, and in 1999 I qualified as a therapist.

Years later, as an older queer Black woman, I've witnessed first-hand the shifts in the LGBTQ+ cultural scene. These shifts have shaped the club I co-run in South Manchester with Vicci Jones, called Stretford Wives. Our events focus on creating a space where connection and community thrive, because what life has taught me is that most of us long for these things.

I've always been captivated by storytelling and the power of drama, though I came to playwriting later than most. In 2021, I joined a short playwriting course with Dibby Theatre. Since then, I've written two short plays – *Unapologetic* and *We See Each Other Better with Our Eyes Closed* (the latter commissioned by the Greater Manchester LGBTQ Culture and Arts Fund). I'm currently working on my third play.

It was through the First Dibs playwriting course that I met Nathaniel and Dibby. When they invited me to support the development of *Toxic*, I was curious. Like many white-led organisations, they talked the talk on diversity, but would they really walk the walk? I'd been disappointed by whiteness before, but I walked toward them with an open heart, willing to give them a chance.

Racism says 'Black is ugly' without proof or right to defend itself, while offering whiteness endless praise. It's an insidious force, and it's why many Black and anti-racism activists are exhausted. A play can entertain, educate, or even transform, but representation aside, I believe the truth is more interesting. I was pleased to see that Nathaniel agreed.

The first draft of *Toxic* presented the white character as the hero/victim and the Black character as the villain. Nathaniel, a passionate activist and social-justice warrior, was committed to challenging these stereotypes, but this initial version still reflected the bias embedded in our society. Even someone deeply concerned with social justice can fall into tired tropes, but Nathaniel acknowledged this challenge head-on, which I deeply respected.

During a community read-through for people of colour and their partners, *we* immediately saw the imbalance. The play, we felt, needed more nuance. I realised that offering this critique could fracture my relationship with Nathaniel. Being honest like that is emotionally taxing, especially for a Black woman, and I've faced consequences for speaking my truth in the past. But I was willing to take that risk because I valued our friendship. To his credit, Nathaniel listened and acknowledged the truth in what we were saying. He rose to the challenge, and Dibby proved they weren't just inviting us to tick boxes – they were committed to action.

As a psychotherapist, I've learned that every person's behaviour has a reason behind it. Good storytelling isn't just about showing what happens but about exploring why. Nathaniel's rewrite showed more than just the surface-level interactions between characters. He dared to expose the flaws beneath the 'pretty white boy' character – those dark, spiteful moments we all can relate to, where pain is inflicted in intimate relationships. He also added depth to the Black character's backstory, providing context for their actions. It didn't completely avoid stereotype, but it gave space for empathy and understanding. When the world treats you badly, sometimes you lash out.

As a white playwright, Nathaniel could have taken the easier route by avoiding writing a Black character in a story about queer domestic abuse. But his willingness to listen and try to understand made all the difference. I admit that some scenes in *Toxic* are still uncomfortable for me to watch, but I know Nathaniel worked hard to make sure the pain of the Black character was felt deeply, particularly when it's rooted in systemic racism and the complications of growing up in a white-dominated world.

The process was raw and emotional for everyone involved. During rehearsals, long, sensitive moments were required to process the pain that the play brought up. The cast used those moments to fuel their performances, producing something truly electrifying.

This experience showed me that not only are Dibby committed to producing work that challenges prejudice, but also that they understand the emotional labour required to truly confront bigotry. Nathaniel, as a writer, showed immense courage in acknowledging that there's a lot he doesn't know. He made himself vulnerable to criticism, and that's where empathy and growth happen.

Through *Toxic*, Nathaniel has written a play that asks difficult questions about intimacy and the barriers to connection, including racism. And by listening to feedback from Black people, he has created a play that whilst full of discomfort, doesn't let white people off the hook.

Racism isn't a 'truth'; it's a lie that deceives us into believing we know each other without truly looking into each other's eyes. Intimacy isn't hard – it's about being seen, speaking your truth in a safe space, and trusting that the exchange is given in good faith. That's where the magic happens.

Toxic offers a glimpse into that magic. It's about queer love, but the themes are universal. It dares to confront racism, wrapped in an evening of humour, drama, movement and music. I feel honoured to have been a part of this process, and I hope the play resonates with you as powerfully as it did with me.

I can think of no better way to celebrate and uplift our community than to dare to listen to each other and learn something, even if doing so is fraught with risk. In my experience, when those conditions are met, magic happens. I laugh louder and deeper. I connect and enter the hidden mysteries of someone else's world. I learn and my spirit expands. There is no greater gift. *Toxic* offers a taste of this, how it is achieved and then how it can be destroyed, and it does so both elegantly and brutally.

Art, in its truest form, should spark conversation and ask tough questions. *Toxic* does just that. It challenges us to really see each other, to take off the masks we wear, and to confront the fragility beneath. In my view, if the world is to reach its beautiful potential, we must learn to 'see' one another fully. *Toxic* takes us one step closer to that understanding.

Susan Kerr is a writer, DJ, events organiser and former psychotherapist.

Acknowledgements

To my partner Seán – thank you for your unwavering love and support. To my family for being the anchor that stopped me drifting away into darkness. And to Josh-Susan Enright – thank you for trusting me with this story and for your vulnerability and bravery to 'go there' in rehearsals and on stage.

To my friends Ciara Tansey and Adam Laidler for your unwavering support for me at both my best and my absolute worst. To Andrew Keates for our late-night chats about shame, addiction and trauma, to Dan Glass for always inspiring me to be bigger, bolder and queerer in my activism, and to Susan Kerr for the emotional labour you invested in challenging my whiteness – when we put down our weapons and dare to really look into one another's eyes, transformation is possible.

To my close team – friend, producer, and fellow Dibby Director Ross Carey, and Amanda Fawcett and Roxanne Carney for stepping in with additional support when we needed it most – thank you.

Further thanks to Emmy Lahouel and Company Chameleon, Waterside Arts, The Met, Superbia at Manchester Pride, staff and services users/clients at George House Trust, Our Room and We Are Survivors, Duncan Craig OBE, participants at workshops and read-throughs, Barry Priest and the GM LGBTQ CAN, Karen O'Neill, Porl Cooper and The Dukes Theatre, Ascension Church, NIAMOS, Manchester Pride, Remi Adefeyisan, Kevin Jamieson, Lisa Allen, Jennie McCusker, Davinia Jokhi, Yvette Sedgeley, Zeph Deakin, the HOME tech and marketing teams, Salford Arts Theatre, New Adelphi Theatre, our touring venues and associated partners, mandla, AJ LeRoy, Sarah Emmott and Art with Heart, Ric Watts, Hollowsphere AV, Nick Hern Books, The White Hotel, and Julie and Iain Herbert.

To all the mega babes who are always on call to answer questions, provide solutions, and offer invaluable insights to help us navigate the challenges of this industry.

And of course – final thanks to Ms Spears for all the bangers.

NJH

A Context

HIV – A Scientific and Sexual Revolution

The play is set during an important time of change in the scientific understanding of HIV.

In 2017, based on findings from multiple research projects across the world, scientists, activists and NGOs gained consensus on what is now known as Undetectable=Untransmittable, or U=U.

Research conclusively confirmed that people with HIV on effective medication, with an 'undetectable' viral load (less than fifty viral copies in 1mL of blood), cannot pass on the virus to others.

Along with increased access to testing and Pre-Exposure Prophylaxis (PrEP), medication taken before sex that offer excellent protection against transmission, U=U has transformed the lives of people living with or affected by HIV.

For more, visit:
www.unaids.org/en/resources/presscentre/featurestories/2018/july/undetectable-untransmittable

Societal Prejudice and Minority Stress

Despite growing acceptance in the UK, LGBTQ+ people are still more likely to experience multiple disadvantages:

- 1 in 3 people with HIV face stigma from their family, friends or workplace (Terrence Higgins Trust)
- Half of LGBTQ+ from the global majority face racism from within the LGBTQ+ community (Stonewall)

- 1 in 4 gay and 1 in 3 bisexual people suffer domestic abuse after age 16 (Stonewall)
- Gay men are 3 times more likely to use illegal substances than heterosexual men (Crime Survey, England and Wales)
- Half of LGBTQ+ people have faced depression, 3 in 5 have faced anxiety (Stonewall)
- 1 in 8 LGBTQ+ people aged 18-24 have attempted to end their life (Stonewall)

Inspired by Nathaniel's lived experience and other stories gathered through outreach, *Toxic* opens a non-judgmental dialogue about the impact of HIV, homophobia, toxic gender norms and racism on queer relationships.

Toxic was first produced by Dibby Theatre and commissioned by HOME. It premiered at HOME, Manchester, on 18 October 2023. It was revived for a UK tour in 2025. The cast was as follows:

THE PLAYWRIGHT	Nathaniel J Hall (He/They)
THE PERFORMER	Josh-Susan Enright (They/Them)
Writer and Creative Lead	Nathaniel J Hall (He/They)
Director	Scott Le Crass (He/Him)
Movement Directors	Plaster Cast: Ayden Brouwers (They/Them) Lizard Morris (They/Them)
Stage Combat (*tour*)	Emmy Lahouel (She/Her)
Designer	Lu Herbert (They/Them)
Composer and Sound Designer	SHAR (Charlotte Barber) (She/Her)
Sound Designer (*original production*)	Joel Clements (He/Him)
Lighting Designer	Tracey Gibbs (She/Her)
Projection Designer	././dede (Dee Dixon) (She/Her)
Dramaturgs	Barry McStay (He/Him) Cheryl Martin (She/Her) Rachel Clements (She/Her) Susan Kerr (She/Her)
Cultural Engagement (*original production*)	Tolu Ajayi (He/They/She) mandla (name as pronouns)
Rehearsal Support (*original production*)	Susan Kerr (She/Her)

Producer	Ross Carey (He/Him)
Associate Producer (*tour*)	Roxanne Carney (She/Her)
Interim Producer (*tour*)	Amanda Fawcett (She/Her)
Production Manager	Joel Clements (He/Him)
Company Stage Manager (*original production*)	Ronly Lam (He/Him)
Company Stage Manager (*tour*)	Amy Tinniswood
Re-lighter (*tour*)	Megan Lucas (She/Her),
Swing Stage Manager (*tour*)	Thomas Kerr (He/Him)
Production Assistant (*original production*)	Ash Cox (She/They)
Rehearsal Room Assistants (*tour*)	Sasha Georgette (She/They) Brit Seaton (She/They)
Accessibility and Inclusion Producer (*tour*)	Ash Cox (She/They)
Set Construction	Ben Cook (He/Him) Simon Pemberton (He/Him)
Scenic Painting	Caitlin Line (She/Her)
Marketing Associate	Natalie Beech (She/Her)
PR Consultant	Rachel Furst (She/Her)
Graphic Designer	Lee Baxter (He/Him)
Trailer Designer	Gavin Wood (He/Him)
Production Photography	Dawn Kilner (She/Her)
Production Videography	Georgiana Ghetiu (She/Her)
BSL Interpreter (*original production*)	Russ Andrews (He/Him)
Captioner (*original production*)	Stevie Burrows (They/Them)
Environmental Consultant	Robin Lyons (He/Him)

The research and development, production and subsequent tour were supported by Arts Council England, the National Lottery Community Fund, the Peggy Ramsay Foundation, We Are Survivors, Superbia at Manchester Pride and The Granada Foundation.

The Dukes Lancaster supported the early development of the play with a seed commission.

The production of this playtext has been supported with sponsorship from ViiV Healthcare.

Characters

THE PLAYWRIGHT, *gay male, white British, early- to mid-thirties, HIV+, a playwright and performer*

THE PERFORMER, *queer, non-binary, mixed heritage (Black Caribbean British father and white British mother), early to mid thirties, HIV–, a dance teacher*

LAKEISHA (*voice-over*), *a middle aged Black British woman, their next door neighbour*

Setting

Manchester.

The play is presented in the present day with flashback to a relationship which spanned 2017–19.

This text went to press before the end of rehearsals and so may differ slightly from the play as performed.

Pre-show: A Big, Messy, Deliciously Dark Night Begins...

On-stage there is a small, square, raked platform set on the diagonal, at the back of which there is a door (stage right) and window frame (stage left) with a smashed pane of glass.

This set piece sits on top of a rectangle of grey floor that juts out towards the audience on the diagonal.

The entire set is concrete, reminiscent of an underground club or warehouse party venue.

Flashes of a typical northern domestic red-brick house show through where the concrete has cracked and fallen off.

But this is no ordinary house, this is a neon party house.

A place and space where the heteronormative is shaken off and the rituals of the queer bacchanal are performed.

A strip of neon light snakes along the back of the platform connecting two microphones set stage left and right.

A metal pendant light hangs over the set.

Two moveable concrete blocks are set on the platform.

Club-level house music pumps out of the speakers.

Smoke and haze fill the stage and the lights gently pulse in anticipation of something about to begin... a big, messy, deliciously dark, night out.

Moment One: A Toxic Prologue

The present moment.

An almighty rush of energy like taking a sniff of poppers.

Projected visuals of pink and yellow pulsate on the set.

And then… that riff.

Instantly recognisable… 'Toxic' by Britney Spears.

But it's remixed – darker, sexier, more dangerous.

THE PLAYWRIGHT *and* THE PERFORMER *appear in front of the microphones.*

They perform a short Britney Spears-inspired routine ending with a concert-style bass drop – boom!

THE PLAYWRIGHT (*speaking on mic*). I couldn't call the show *Toxic* and not start with that could I?

THE PERFORMER (*on mic*). Yeah, that would have been homophobic.

THE PLAYWRIGHT (*commanding*). This is the story of how we met, fell in love and fucked it up.

THE PERFORMER. But it's not just our story.

THE PLAYWRIGHT. It's his, and his… and theirs.

THE PERFORMER. Maybe it's yours.

THE PLAYWRIGHT. Maybe.

THE PERFORMER. Most of what you're about to see tonight *is* true.

THE PLAYWRIGHT. Every pill popped, every face snogged, every line snorted, every cock sucked, every slur shouted, every fist raised happened… to someone.

THE PERFORMER. Oh, it's gonna be a laugh a minute.

THE PLAYWRIGHT. We don't have names.

THE PERFORMER. Because it's better when it's anonymous.

THE PLAYWRIGHT. So, let's just call me 'The Playwright'.

THE PERFORMER. And I'm 'The Performer'.

THE PLAYWRIGHT. And we're here to tell you a story about two lovers –

THE PERFORMER. Ex-lovers.

THE PLAYWRIGHT. They met in Manchester in late 2017.

THE PERFORMER. That's important.

THE PLAYWRIGHT. The year.

THE PERFORMER. Because a revolution was taking place.

THE PLAYWRIGHT. Not on the streets.

But in our bodies.

THE PERFORMER. And in the sheets.

THE PLAYWRIGHT. PrEP and U=U.

New science, new drug trials, revolutionising the sex people like us could have.

THE PERFORMER. Removing fear and smashing the stigma.

THE PLAYWRIGHT. Sort of.

We're not *actually* ex-lovers.

THE PERFORMER. But from here on in, you need to pretend we are.

THE PLAYWRIGHT. Some of what you're about to see is proper heavy.

THE PERFORMER. And you may need to take a break.

THE PLAYWRIGHT. That's okay.

THE PERFORMER. Sometimes survival means knowing when to leave.

THE PLAYWRIGHT. And remember, we only do this out of love.

THE PERFORMER. For you.

THE PLAYWRIGHT. For us.... for *all* of us.

THE PERFORMER. Well, shall we tell the goddamn thing then?

THE PLAYWRIGHT. Let's get this party started.

So, this is the story of how we met, fell in love –

THE PLAYWRIGHT *and* THE PERFORMER (*together, shouting obnoxiously*). – and fucked it up!

Moment Two: Blanche Hooks Up With Dorothy

The present moment, with flashback to the gay hook-up app, Grindr, autumn 2017.

Upbeat house music plays, something with drive and movement.

A short dance sequence.

THE PLAYWRIGHT *and* THE PERFORMER *dress each other in shirts to become the two lovers.*

THE PLAYWRIGHT *gets two mobile phones and passes one to* THE PERFORMER *with a wink: let's go!*

In the mix we hear the unmistakable sound of the Grindr message tone.

They smile knowingly at the audience.

Another burst of movement with the phones.

THE PLAYWRIGHT *appears in the doorway posing for his profile photo – the phone lights up his face.*

The following text is read by an electronic screen reader (ESR) with each character voiced by a different electronic voice.

The text is animated via projections across the set.

Typing, swiping and message tone sound effects complete the effect.

THE PLAYWRIGHT (ESR). The curious boy conquers the (s)ass

Thirty-one

He/Him

Versatile

HIV Status: HIV+

Looking for: Mr Right, Mr Right Now

Sounds of typing and then THE PERFORMER *appears in the doorway posing for their profile photo – the phone lights their face.*

THE PERFORMER (ESR). Come feel my bump and grind boi

Thirty

They/Them

Versatile

HIV Status: HIV– (on PrEP)

Looking for: masc4mascara

A Grindr message tone.

Throughout the following we hear the relevant sending and receiving sounds for each message.

THE PLAYWRIGHT (ESR). Fit.

THE PERFORMER (ESR). Thanks.

A pause for typing.

On screen we see an animated ellipsis (…) with relevant sound effect (this is repeated wherever 'pause for typing' or (…) is written).

THE PERFORMER (ESR). Also fit (aubergine emoji, squirt emoji).

A pause for typing (…).

THE PLAYWRIGHT (ESR). Thanks (wink emoji (…) tongue emoji, aubergine emoji, peach emoji, squirt emoji (…) smirk emoji).

A pause for typing (…).

THE PERFORMER (ESR). Wanna meet up?

THE PLAYWRIGHT (ESR). I'm at work (sad-face emoji).

THE PERFORMER (ESR). Send pics.

THE PLAYWRIGHT *flicks through his phone and sends the pics – three photos, sexy but all clothed.*

A pause for typing (…).

THE PERFORMER (ESR). I meant dick pics (laughing emoji).

THE PLAYWRIGHT (ESR). Or maybe we could go on a journey of discovery together?

I'm just traditional like that (married couple emoji).

THE PERFORMER (ESR). Sure, Jan (smirk emoji).

A pause for typing (…).

THE PLAYWRIGHT (ESR) *and* THE PERFORMER (ESR) (*together*). What you into?

A pause for typing (…).

THE PERFORMER (ESR). Hard bareback sex (devil emoji).

THE PLAYWRIGHT (ESR). Watching reruns of *The Golden Girls* with a G and T (G and T emoji).

A pause for typing (…).

I like your idea too (devil emoji).

THE PERFORMER (ESR). And I LOVE *The Golden Girls* (smile emoji).

THE PLAYWRIGHT (ESR). Really!?

> Maybe we can shag then watch Betty White and the girls together after... CAMP.
>
> *A pause for typing (...)*
>
> *A really long pause!*
>
> Too much?

THE PERFORMER (ESR). I'm more of a Blanche than a Rose (heel emoji).

THE PLAYWRIGHT (ESR). I'm definitely a Dorothy.

> She's done with the world.
>
> Hard relate.

THE PERFORMER (ESR). You're funny.

> Different.
>
> I like it (squirt emoji, squirt emoji, squirt emoji).
>
> Not like the usual trash on here.
>
> *They turn to look at one another.*

THE PLAYWRIGHT (ESR). Want to take the trash out with me Blanche?

THE PERFORMER (ESR). I thought you'd never ask, Dorothy.

> *And the messaging is over.*
>
> *They put the phones away.*
>
> *A burst of movement.*

Moment Three: Are You Even Gay Though?

Autumn 2017, mid-afternoon. A café in Manchester.

They move the stage blocks to create two seats in a café.

THE PERFORMER *is sat down waiting for their date to arrive and as the movement sequence ends,* THE PLAYWRIGHT, *slightly breathless, lands in the other seat.*

THE PLAYWRIGHT. Sorry, train was late.

THE PERFORMER. Nice of you to make it, Dorothy.

THE PLAYWRIGHT. And turning up for a first date hungover, not a great look, I'm aware.

THE PERFORMER. Who says I'm not hungover too?

A pause – THE PLAYWRIGHT *contemplates: are they joking or not?*

Who says I've even been to bed?

A pause – THE PLAYWRIGHT *still can't decide if they're joshing him or not.*

THE PLAYWRIGHT. And here's me feeling bad because I had one too many tequilas at Sandra's leaving do last night.

THE PERFORMER. I find a light powder of the nose can help with that.

THE PLAYWRIGHT. Not sure Sandra from finance is into Class As, babes. Mind you, never really thought to ask.

THE PERFORMER. It's always the quiet ones.

THE PLAYWRIGHT. I love a good party, but I don't really go in hard for it.

THE PERFORMER. You're telling me you've never had a line?

THE PLAYWRIGHT. Well... yeah.

I'm a gay man in my thirties; did Mother Teresa ever go to confession?

THE PERFORMER. What about pills?

THE PLAYWRIGHT *shakes his head*.

Ketamine?

G?

MDMA?

Weed?

THE PLAYWRIGHT *is still shaking his head*.

Jeez, even me nan's smoked a spliff.

I'm supposed to be cutting back personally, but, well, Christmas soon, innit?

THE PLAYWRIGHT. Actually, I tried weed at uni once but had a whitey and vomited on a fresher's dick.

A pause – was that the right thing to say on a first date?

Sorry, I just get a bit nervous when I meet people for the first time.

THE PERFORMER. You weren't nervous when you sent me a photo of your cock last week.

THE PLAYWRIGHT. Well, no.

THE PERFORMER. So, relax.

THE PLAYWRIGHT. Yeah, last night's beer-fear is really kicking in now.

A pause.

THE PERFORMER (*to the server*). Glass of white wine, please.

THE PLAYWRIGHT (*to the server*). Oh, erm, just a coffee for me, thanks.

THE PERFORMER. You've genuinely never had a pill on a night out?

THE PLAYWRIGHT (*laughing*). No.

I don't know, it's complicated.

THE PERFORMER. Ooh, red flag!

You must know you're not supposed to say 'it's complicated' on a first date.

THE PLAYWRIGHT. It hardly feels like a first date given that we've –

THE PERFORMER (*interrupting*) – already wanked over each other's pics?

THE PLAYWRIGHT. Yeah.

I guess that's the gay way to say hello… shake hands.

THE PERFORMER. Well, thank you for shaking my –

THE PLAYWRIGHT. – hand.

If that's the handshake, then what does a first date entail?

THE PERFORMER. I dunno, gangbang?

THE PLAYWRIGHT. I don't think my nerves could take it.

I prefer things more one-on-one anyway.

THE PERFORMER. So, you've never been to a gang bang either?

THE PLAYWRIGHT. Oh, God no.

THE PERFORMER. Sex party?

THE PLAYWRIGHT *shakes his head again*.

Sauna?

Nope.

Threesome?

Nope.

THE PERFORMER. Oh my God, are you even gay?

Right, I need to check your gay credentials immediately.

THE PLAYWRIGHT. Okay?

THE PERFORMER. Answer at gay walking pace.

THE PLAYWRIGHT *looks confused*.

(*Exasperated*.) Fast!

Okay, favourite colour?

THE PLAYWRIGHT. Pink.

THE PERFORMER. Camp.

Favourite TV show?

THE PLAYWRIGHT. *The Golden Girls*.

THE PERFORMER. Obvs.

Favourite film?

THE PLAYWRIGHT. *First Wives Club*.

THE PERFORMER. Divine.

Favourite food?

THE PLAYWRIGHT. Curry, but not if I'm bottom.

THE PERFORMER. Sensible.

Favourite sports team?

THE PLAYWRIGHT *hesitates*.

Right answer.

Favourite Britney song?

THE PLAYWRIGHT. Erm… 'Until the World Ends'… underrated bop.

THE PERFORMER. Ahh, mine's 'Toxic'.

THE PLAYWRIGHT (*teasing*). Oh, red flag.

Look, I'm not a nun or anything!

It's just sex… it's complicated for me.

THE PERFORMER. There's that word again.

THE PLAYWRIGHT. My first time wasn't great, that's all.

THE PERFORMER. Whose was?

THE PLAYWRIGHT. My first-time story is definitely more like second date material.

THE PERFORMER. If you make it that far.

THE PLAYWRIGHT (*hesitant*). Well, you know my HIV status, right?

THE PERFORMER. Told you, doesn't bother me… and I'm on PrEP.

THE PLAYWRIGHT. Well… I got it… from my first…

THE PERFORMER *contemplates before the penny drops.*

THE PERFORMER. Oh babe, talk about unlucky.

I'm so sorry.

THE PLAYWRIGHT. Don't be.

It's ancient history.

And I'm undetectable which means –

THE PERFORMER. – you're untransmittable.

THE PLAYWRIGHT *looks pleasantly surprised that they know this information.*

THE PLAYWRIGHT. Yeah.

It's all a bit new, though, and I'm not sure how I feel about it all, but yeah.

THE PERFORMER. If it's any consolation my childhood was a fucking shit show.

Mum found out she was pregnant with me in the Asda toilet after a big weekend, talk about a come down.

Every time I walk past one of them yellow sticker things, I can't help thinking that I'm the biggest 'whoopsie' of the lot.

It was all downhill from there really.

THE PLAYWRIGHT *laughs and then stares at* THE PERFORMER *smiling.*

What!?

THE PLAYWRIGHT. You're a wrong'un…

THE PERFORMER. Blanche is an acquired taste, that's for sure.

A pause.

(*Leaning in, a loud whisper.*) You mean to say you got HIV at sixteen and you didn't end up a messy chemsex queen?

You actually must be Mother Teresa.

THE PLAYWRIGHT (*laughing*). I mean, I can't say I haven't ever been tempted to party a bit harder.

THE PERFORMER. What about now?

There's this amazing night tonight at Hidden, the best queer party in the country, hands down.

(*Teasing.*) I was going to go with another guy I've been chatting with, but you know, he's not as cute as you.

How about shaking off that hangover with me?

It's okay, I'm not a drug pusher or anything.

I know a guy.

And you can try some if you like or pass if not.

But I would really like to dance with you tonight either way.

THE PLAYWRIGHT. I'm hungover.

THE PERFORMER. Hair of the dog?

I promise I'll look after you.

THE PLAYWRIGHT *considers it*.

THE PLAYWRIGHT. Oh my God, this is crazy.

You're crazy.

THE PERFORMER. Maybe… just don't hold it against me.

THE PLAYWRIGHT. Till the world ends.

Moment Four: A Mad, Drug-Fuelled, Sexy Macarena

The same evening and into the next morning. An alleyway, a bar and an underground queer club.

A burst of 'Crazy' by Britney Spears kicks off a pulsing soundscape that takes us on a journey through different places.

Another duet – they clear away the café in a slick choreographed routine.

Occasionally they brush against one another or catch each other's eyes, lingering and enjoying these moments of connection.

A brief moment in an alleyway: THE PERFORMER *scores drugs whilst* THE PLAYWRIGHT *keeps lookout – they both inhale deeply through their nostrils again.*

They enter a busy bar.

A chair duet – they drink and talk and drink and talk and sniff and talk and drink and talk.

Closer, closer, closer… but no kiss yet.

They both take a pill.

They throw off their coats as they enter a new place – Hidden night club.

A burst of smoke as they arrive in the club, the queer bacchanalia.

Arms and armpits and painted faces, glitter and leather and lace and chains fill the space.

They dance seductively across the dance floor.

THE PERFORMER *offers* THE PLAYWRIGHT *another pill.*

They place one in each other's mouths, so close they almost kiss… but not yet.

And then they're in the smoking area.

THE PERFORMER *smokes a cigarette*, THE PLAYWRIGHT *stares into space.*

The beat from inside the club morphs into a techno version of 'The Macarena'.

THE PLAYWRIGHT *comes up hard and fast – we have to dance, NOW!*

And they do.

Everything glistens and glitters, lights strobe.

They dance 'The Macarena' – a mad, silly, sexy, drug fuelled Macarena.

And then, everything falls away and it's just them, staring into one another's eyes.

They are falling, deep, deep, deep into one another, moving closer, closer, so, so close… and touchdown!

They kiss.

A deep, passionate, sweaty, middle-of-the-dancefloor, total centre-of-the-universe kiss.

The club fades away, only they matter or even exist right now.

THE PLAYWRIGHT *takes out a condom from his pocket, but* THE PERFORMER *takes it from him and throws it away.*

THE PERFORMER (*mouths*). Fuck me.

They both run to the microphones frantically undressing themselves in the process, and we hear them having sex amplified by the mic – powerful, strong, intense, sensual.

The music climaxes, as do they, followed by heavy breathing and post-coital smiling, release.

They begin to get dressed.

Oh my God I've just remembered!

It wasn't just the Macarena, you twerked right in the middle of the dancefloor.

THE PLAYWRIGHT. Shit, was that cultural approps?

36   TOXIC

THE PERFORMER. Just really bad dancing, babes.

That white batty really can't twerk.

THE PLAYWRIGHT. I am so glad you didn't 'cancel' me.

THE PERFORMER. For having your ass in the air?

Never.

Moment Five: A Trauma Bond So Tight

Anywhere and nowhere, a liminal time and place.

Soft, expansive music reverberates through the space, projected visuals and light flicker, nostalgic, like watching an old film with rose-tinted glasses.

They sit on the front point of the rosta, backs together but facing away from one another.

THE PERFORMER (*on mic*). When he told me his story
   And we realised
   It was his first time
   Without
   The need
   For protection
   No risk of rejection
   For being
   One hundred per cent true
   Fully you equals you
   And me
   Free
   A chance for skin
   To penetrate skin
   Deep within
   A seed
   That breeds

    A unity so tight
    So intoxicating
    It might
    Just
    Fix
    Everything.

THE PLAYWRIGHT (*on mic*). When they told me their story
    Of not being quite
    White enough
    Or Black enough
    Or masc enough
    Or femme enough
    A constant shift
    On a fictional binary
    Adrift
    With no anchor
    Only the memory
    Of a father figure
    And a thousand
    Notches in the bedpost
    A ghost
    Of your former self
    Stuck in cycles
    Of self-sabotage
    I wanted to smother you
    Cover you
    Hold you and never
    Let
    You
    Go.

THE PERFORMER. When he told me his story

THE PLAYWRIGHT *and* THE PERFORMER (*together*). Fuck me

THE PLAYWRIGHT. It felt

    Like every part of me

THE PERFORMER. Every part of him

> Fused
>
> A bond so tight

THE PLAYWRIGHT. We thought that it might

> Smash the very atoms of our beings
>
> Into one.

THE PERFORMER. And we tried

> We willed our bodies and our souls
>
> Together
>
> Two halves
>
> Separated
>
> Desperate to become one

THE PLAYWRIGHT. Banging and smashing together

THE PERFORMER. So hard

THE PLAYWRIGHT. Trying to fill holes

> To make ourselves whole.

THE PLAYWRIGHT *and* THE PERFORMER (*together*). When you told me your story

> When you gave me that piece of you
>
> That was special
>
> No one else could ever share that bond

THE PLAYWRIGHT. Ours

THE PERFORMER. Mine

THE PLAYWRIGHT. Yours

THE PERFORMER. Mine

THE PLAYWRIGHT. Yours

> I'm all yours

THE PERFORMER. Just you and me

    Facing eternity

    Together

THE PLAYWRIGHT. No one can harm us here.

THE PERFORMER. Bonded.

THE PLAYWRIGHT. Glued.

THE PERFORMER. Complete.

THE PLAYWRIGHT. No more holes.

THE PERFORMER. No more leaking.

THE PLAYWRIGHT. Two halves.

THE PLAYWRIGHT *and* THE PERFORMER (*together*). Made whole.

Moment Six: It's My Birthday, I'll Cry If I Want To

Spring 2018. The living room of a typical Manchester terraced house.

They begin moving into their new home.

THE PLAYWRIGHT *grabs a carboard box and begins emptying it.*

THE PLAYWRIGHT. We moved fast.

THE PERFORMER. I'd been bumming it around Manchester after a gig, so without a proper place to call home, I just started spending time at his.

THE PLAYWRIGHT. And my housemates were not happy with the arrangement so a few months in, we got our own place.

THE PERFORMER. Decorated it –

THE PLAYWRIGHT. – even though it was rented.

THE PLAYWRIGHT *pulls out a Bakelite-type phone and passes it to* THE PERFORMER *who looks at it disapprovingly.*

He plugs it in.

THE PERFORMER. Got a car.

THE PLAYWRIGHT. Got a dog.

THE PERFORMER (*pulling two cushions out of the box*). Got a sofa on finance from DFS.

THE PLAYWRIGHT. Bonded over our love of mid-century modern and MDMA.

They move the stage blocks centre and put the cushions on top to make a sofa.

THE PERFORMER. God if that sofa could talk.

THE PLAYWRIGHT. Babes, it can't walk, the pounding we gave it.

We worked hard.

THE PERFORMER. And we partied harder.

THE PLAYWRIGHT. And when the comedowns got too much, we did wholesome activities like walking in the Peak District.

THE PERFORMER. That's a lie.

THE PLAYWRIGHT. Yeah, that's a lie we called the dealer.

They sit look at one another settled in their new home and life together.

THE PLAYWRIGHT *and* THE PERFORMER (*together*). It felt like we had it all.

THE PLAYWRIGHT. And then my best friend Danny died, suddenly.

THE PERFORMER. You mean ex-shag.

THE PLAYWRIGHT. Found dead in his bed after a night out.

THE PERFORMER (*sort of joking*). Yeah, the night before my birthday, the inconsiderate shit.

They pull out a party banner that reads 'Happy Birthday!' and string it across the stage.

Two wine glasses appear out of the box.

THE PLAYWRIGHT. The day after we found out, my best friend Stacey came over, she knew Danny too.

And we cooked a nice meal and tried to make the effort for your birthday, but we were both just totally shell-shocked.

They sit in silence in the dining room sipping wine.

Music can be heard quietly playing from a speaker in the background – Britney Spears' Greatest Hits.

THE PERFORMER (*breaking the silence*). You know, I think I'd be more upset if the dog died than you.

Silence.

It was just a joke.

I'm just trying to lighten the mood; you know it is supposed to be a birthday party.

An uneasy silence descends again.

After a long pause, the phone rings loudly.

They both jump.

I thought you said you'd fixed that stupid thing.

THE PLAYWRIGHT *goes to pick up the phone listens to check there is no one there and puts it down.*

Why do we even have one anyway?

We never use it, and it keeps ringing when nobody's calling, it's like something from a horror film, creeps me out.

THE PLAYWRIGHT. I dunno, it's just kitsch, I guess.

THE PERFORMER. If it's just for the gram, why is it plugged in?

THE PLAYWRIGHT. I don't know, for emergencies?

I like to have a landline connection to my mum, just in case.

THE PERFORMER. The mum who you've still not told you have HIV.

THE PLAYWRIGHT. Oh, classy.

THE PERFORMER. I just say it as I see it.

If that thing rang and it was my mum, I wouldn't just jump out my skin, I'd have a coronary.

THE PLAYWRIGHT. Well at least you'd be able to call an ambulance to come and save you.

A pause.

THE PERFORMER *probes further, they really don't like landline phones for some reason.*

THE PERFORMER. Hang on, if there was an emergency, you'd have your mobile on you, wouldn't you?

You're never off the damn thing.

And who are you calling in this emergency?

The police?

THE PLAYWRIGHT. If I needed the police I'd call the police, yeah.

THE PERFORMER. And what possible scenario would lead to you not having your mobile and needing to call the police on the landline?

THE PLAYWRIGHT. Oh, I don't know…

You've just smashed my phone in an uncontrollable jealous rage after you saw the fit postie give me a compliment?

THE PERFORMER *looks less than impressed.*

I'm kidding, it was just a joke.

And the postie's straight, no gay man would be seen dead in knee-length cargo shorts.

Why is this such a big deal for you?

THE PERFORMER (*lying*). It's not… I'm just curious.

A pause.

I still think we should get rid of it.

People only ever ring you on the landline if it's bad news and quite frankly I've had enough of that for a lifetime –

THE PLAYWRIGHT. – fine!

I'll throw it in the bin if it will shut you up for just five minutes!

They go back to sitting in silence.

THE PERFORMER (*drunk, sarcastic*). Well, happy birthday to me!

A clunk like a mic cable has been unplugged.

A quiet sort of 'white noise' and the sound of a phone off the hook.

It jars with the music coming from the speaker.

The pendant light flickers.

Something is beginning to creak under its own weight, something that's going to fracture spectacularly in due course.

THE PLAYWRIGHT. Don't say that.

THE PERFORMER. What?

I'm just trying to lighten the mood.

And the red wine had gone straight to our heads, and you said:

THE PLAYWRIGHT. Lighten the mood?

Our friend has just died.

THE PERFORMER. It's still my birthday.

THE PLAYWRIGHT. Yeah, and you'll live to see your next one as well.

And you threw down your napkin, shoved the table and said:

THE PERFORMER. Fucking shit birthday party this, you could have at least tried.

THE PLAYWRIGHT. If it's that fucking shit, why are you still here?

A silent stand-off.

THE PERFORMER *storms out of the door – an adult tantrum from a childhood wound.*

(*Looking up, then to Stacey.*) Bloody bulbs going an' all.

Proper house of horrors, this place.

THE PERFORMER *enters behind the set.*

THE PERFORMER. Alexa, play 'Crazy' by Britney Spears.

'Crazy' by Britney Spears plays loudly.

THE PERFORMER *dances, drunk, and pretends to be having a good time but underneath they are crumbling.*

THE PLAYWRIGHT (*shouting through the door*). For God's sake will you turn that down?

What a fucking day, hey?

THE PERFORMER *hesitates, then turns it off to make a point and an uneasy truce descends.*

Suddenly, the phone rings loudly.

THE PLAYWRIGHT *gets up and goes to answer it.*

We hear it click to connect as he puts it to his ear.

Through the phone we hear his voice.

Here comes the bit where it hurts.

The phone disconnects and the dial tone echoes.

He stares at the receiver.

A rush of something overwhelming, a club riser and a final flourish of Ms Spears' vocals: 'CRAAAAZZYY!'

A concert-style bass drop as he slams the phone on the hook.

Moment Seven: Spit In My Face, Part 1

Summer 2018. The living room of their terraced house.

THE PLAYWRIGHT *and* THE PERFORMER *are returning home in the early hours wearing pink tacky hen do gear. As they walk down the street* THE PERFORMER *sings Britney songs loudly.*

They arrive through the doorway into the living room and have a hard passionate snog in the doorway.

They're high and horny… really horny.

THE PLAYWRIGHT. Alexa, play high and horny mix.

They strip off as they speak.

I'm so glad we left; I couldn't wait to leave and get my hands on you.

THE PERFORMER. Yeah, and Ste's new boyfriend's teeth were sending me under.

THE PLAYWRIGHT *sticks his teeth out mocking Ste's boyfriend.*

They've got to be falsies… they look like they're from Porcelanosa.

THE PERFORMER *also sticks their teeth out in a mocking grin, and they dance towards one another in a mock sexy way.*

THE PLAYWRIGHT (*through toothy grin*). I have never been more attracted to you than right now.

They come together in a passionate embrace, removing some clothing.

They run to the the microphones and perform the fucking in an abstract manner as they did earlier.

Their sex sounds echo and reverberate through the soundscape.

Yeaahhh, you like that?

THE PERFORMER. Yeah.

THE PLAYWRIGHT. Take it like a fucking bitch!

THE PERFORMER. Oh, oh, oh, oh.

THE PLAYWRIGHT. Oh my God!

THE PERFORMER. Spit on me!

Spit on me!

Go on, do it.

I consent!

THE PLAYWRIGHT *spits and* THE PERFORMER *loves it.*

Ohhhhhhh, yes!

Do it again!

In my face!

THE PLAYWRIGHT *spits again.*

Yeah, yeah, yeah!

THE PLAYWRIGHT. Dirty fucking animal.

THE PERFORMER. Let me do it to you.

THE PLAYWRIGHT (*reluctant*). Erm, yeah okay.

THE PERFORMER *spits*.

(*Surprised*.) Oh my God that's actually good.

THE PERFORMER. So good.

The doorbell rings.

Suddenly the shine of being high and horny disappears but they try to continue.

Ignore it, don't stop.

The doorbell rings again.

THE PLAYWRIGHT. Fucks sake.

THE PERFORMER. Don't stop, don't stop, pleeeaaase don't stop.

It rings over and over.

THE PLAYWRIGHT. Fuck!

They stop, dressing gowns go on.

The sound of the front door opening.

LAKEISHA (*voice-over*). Hiya is everything alright?

Just I heard quite a lot of noise and commotion.

THE PLAYWRIGHT. It's Lakeisha, heart of gold, but she works at a shelter for abused women, and you can't say boo to a goose without her checking in.

(*To Lakeisha*.) Everything's fine Lakeisha, we're just moving some furniture about, you know spring clean and all that.

LAKEISHA (*voice-over*). At five o'clock in the morning?

It's just I thought I heard someone shout, 'please don't spit on my face' and I just wanted to check you were both alright.

THE PLAYWRIGHT. Really!?

God, these walls!

I said: 'don't spit on it… you… nutcase… we've got some polish!'

Everything's fine, honestly.

The sound of the front door closing.

THE PERFORMER (*on mic*). Okay, where were we?

THE PLAYWRIGHT (*on mic*). I think you were spitting in my face.

THE PERFORMER. Yeah.

(*A chant, sexy, silly*). Spit – in – yer – face!
Spit – in – yer – face!
Spit – in – yer – face!

THE PLAYWRIGHT. I'll spit on Lakeisha's face!

Nosy fucking cow.

Can you hear us, Lakeisha?

THE PLAYWRIGHT *makes loud, grotesque over the top sex noises.*

THE PERFORMER *joins in.*

The beat swells towards a climax.

The energy of the high pulses back into their bodies.

Yes! Yes! Yes! I'm ready, are you ready? Oh, oh, oh!

And they've come.

Moment Eight: Pillow Talk

The morning after. The bedroom of their terraced house.

THE PLAYWRIGHT *and* THE PERFORMER *are lying about in the post drug-fuck afterglow.*

THE PLAYWRIGHT. I've never done that.

The spitting thing.

THE PERFORMER. Didn't you like it?

THE PLAYWRIGHT. I loved it.

Is that weird?

THE PERFORMER. I don't think so, as long as we're *both* enjoying it.

THE PLAYWRIGHT. I never even thought I'd be able to have sex without a condom and look at me now.

THE PERFORMER. Did it feel good?

THE PLAYWRIGHT. Yeah.

THE PERFORMER. So?

Punishment is pleasure, humans are weird, and you're a kinky bastard.

THE PLAYWRIGHT. You do know you're my first time without condoms, since –

THE PERFORMER. Like your first time all over again.

THE PLAYWRIGHT *doesn't say anything*.

Well, I am honoured to be the one to take your bareback virginity.

THE PLAYWRIGHT. Don't.

THE PERFORMER. What?

THE PLAYWRIGHT. That word.

THE PERFORMER. Bareback?

THE PLAYWRIGHT. It makes me shudder.

THE PERFORMER. But that's 'our thing'.

A pause.

I guess I never really thought about how hard it must be until I met you.

I just thought you took a pill a day and that's it.

THE PLAYWRIGHT. If it were that simple, I would've told my parents years ago.

I remember at school we were shown this film about AIDS in PSHE, with this gay guy in his twenties who had been diagnosed with HIV... he was basically dying.

The message was clear as day: 'Don't be gay, you will get AIDS and die.'

Like Coach Carr in *Mean Girls*, but not funny.

I sat there with twenty-seven pairs of eyes burning in the back of my neck, trying not to flinch, desperately thinking, 'don't let them see you are one of *them.*'

Anyway, the prophecy came true two years later... gay and HIV+ at sweet sixteen.

He was a lot older than me, and I trusted him.

Got high with his mate a few times, my middle-class rebellion.

Blacked out once.

THE PERFORMER. Did they...?

THE PLAYWRIGHT. No, I don't think so... I don't know, it was a long time ago.

When I was diagnosed, the clinic insisted I give them a landline number.

I was so scared they might ring and tell my mum and dad, so I gave them the wrong one.

THE PERFORMER. Which explains why you jump every time the phone rings.

They both half-laugh.

Did you ever think it might be just easier to find someone else living with it?

THE PLAYWRIGHT (*sarcastic, playful*). Maybe we can pop a pink triangle on all of us and put us in a camp?

Oh, come on, how would you feel if I asked you if you had thought about only dating Black boys?

THE PERFORMER (*suddenly defensive*). Nah, that's totally different.

And I'm not Black, I'm mixed, it's different.

THE PLAYWRIGHT. I know you are.

THE PERFORMER. I just meant it might be easier if you both had it.

THE PLAYWRIGHT. There's websites for that.

THE PERFORMER. There's websites for everything, babes.

Just type 'ebony gay porn' into google.

I still can't believe they call it that.

It's alright for you, you fit the gay-scene mould perfectly.

THE PLAYWRIGHT. That's unfair.

THE PERFORMER. Have you ever been searched for drugs at a club whilst all your white friends get waved through?

THE PLAYWRIGHT. Has anyone ever told you they don't want to fuck you because you're 'infected with AIDS'?

A pause – THE PERFORMER *attempts to diffuse the tension.*

THE PERFORMER (*singing*). Intoxicate me now, with your lovin' now.

THE PLAYWRIGHT (*smiling*). You're not right in the head, you.

THE PERFORMER (*grinning*). Don't hold it against me.

Oh my God, can you believe this one time, this white guy asked me to be his slave?

THE PLAYWRIGHT. Fuck off!

THE PERFORMER. I told him I was going to screenshot it and post it on Twitter.

THE PLAYWRIGHT. You little fucker!

THE PERFORMER. I know.

THE PLAYWRIGHT. Someone begged me to give them my poz load once.

I screamed and ran a mile.

THE PERFORMER. It's the wild west out there, babes.

THE PLAYWRIGHT. Tell me about it.

THE PERFORMER. I am so glad I have found you.

THE PLAYWRIGHT. Same.

THE PERFORMER. To not being a twat.

THE PLAYWRIGHT. To not being racist.

THE PERFORMER. To not being… virophobic?

THE PLAYWRIGHT. That's good enough for me.

To being seen.

THE PERFORMER. To being seen.

THE PLAYWRIGHT. To being spit on.

THE PERFORMER. To our thing.

THE PLAYWRIGHT. Till the world ends.

They kiss.

Moment Nine: Marry Me?

Late-summer 2018. A fancy restaurant, Manchester.

A brief duet – they dress for dinner setting the restaurant up in the process.

THE PLAYWRIGHT *passes* THE PERFORMER *a restaurant menu as they land in their seats and sit reading them.*

THE PERFORMER. Well, this is nice, we've not had a proper date night in ages.

THE PLAYWRIGHT. I never really made up for Danny popping his clogs on your birthday, so consider this your belated birthday present.

And it's Pride this weekend, so we're starting the celebrations in style.

THE PERFORMER. I'm not going wild this weekend babes, you know it's bad for my head.

THE PLAYWRIGHT (*teasing*). Oh, look who's Mother Teresa now.

They read their menus.

THE PERFORMER *notices something happening on the other side of the restaurant.*

THE PERFORMER. You know, the waiter has completely ignored that Black couple since we arrived, fucking prick.

THE PLAYWRIGHT. It's busy, it's probably not intentional.

THE PERFORMER (*irritated, sarcastic*). Thank God I have a white mum *and* a white boyfriend; I'd be starving right now if it wasn't for you.

THE PLAYWRIGHT. Babes, please don't start, I just want us to have a nice time, please?

A pause – tension lingers in the air.

You never really talk about her.

THE PERFORMER. Sandra?

THE PLAYWRIGHT. Yeah, and your dad.

A pause.

THE PERFORMER. Sandra liked hanging out at shebeens because she had a 'thing' for black guys.

THE PLAYWRIGHT. Shebeen?

THE PERFORMER. It's like an underground club, there were loads in London in the eighties.

That's where she met Devon – one night stand, Brixton, 1985.

THE PLAYWRIGHT. Ouch.

THE PERFORMER. To be fair they did give it a shot when they found out she was pregnant and it wasn't a totally shit childhood, at least not the first part.

We didn't have money to burn but at Christmas we'd do that thing every kid in the nineties did, you know, circle what we wanted in the Argos catalogue.

I remember this one year Devon traipsed every shop to find me a Furby, but I drowned it on New Year's Eve because the little shit wouldn't shut up.

THE PLAYWRIGHT. Precisely the reason why *we* were never allowed one.

THE PERFORMER (*referring to the Black couple*). What's happening over there, the waiter ignoring thing, something like that would have set Devon right off.

He spat in a man's face on a flight to Alicante once, but that *was* deserved because he said our lot were more suited to travelling on ships, racist prick.

THE PLAYWRIGHT. Jesus.

THE PERFORMER. He used to tell me all these stories about how he'd been on the frontline at the Brixton uprisings.

Sandra always corrected him, 'riots, Devon, they were riots', she'd say.

It's not that she didn't see the racism, she just chose to ignore it.

Her response was always, 'just rise above it, be the bigger man.'

Anyway, I learned it was better to stay out of the line of fire pretty quickly.

THE PLAYWRIGHT. Sometimes survival means knowing when to leave.

THE PERFORMER. Yeah, except as a kid you can't leave, can you?

Despite her respectable demeanour in public, Sandra was a proper firecracker behind closed doors, especially when she'd had a drink.

This one night I heard her threaten to call the police if he dare lay a finger on her.

The day after, he sat me down.

'Just because you got a white mum, don't you think for a second they don't see you differently, boy.'

'Don't think they won't arrest now, think later.'

I was ten.

THE PLAYWRIGHT. Did he ever... [hit her]?

THE PERFORMER. Babes they both gave as good each other, but threatening a Black man, your own partner, with the police?

Nah, that's a step too far.

Anyway, it's like time sped up after that.

The headteacher found me in the girl's toilets dressed as Ursula from *The Little Mermaid* and the social got involved and it was a whole big thing.

Not because of the cross-dressing, that blew over, but because every time someone came round, they were at each other's throats.

I remember one of the social workers asking me if any men in my family had been giving me special presents, the shame.

I told them my dad bought me a Furby once, but I drowned it.

They both laugh and the tension releases a bit.

I reckon he was in trouble with the police, you know, from the rio– the uprisings.

And I think Sandra wanted to appease the social, in case any of that came up, but Devon was having none of it.

Then, the night before my eleventh birthday they had this blazing row, stuff smashing everywhere, and the next day he was gone.

One day I had a dad, the next day I didn't.

THE PLAYWRIGHT. When you kicked off on your birthday, Stacey said you were a nutcase, and I should run a mile.

THE PERFORMER. I was a dick that night.

THE PLAYWRIGHT. Yeah, you were, but at least now I understand why.

THE PERFORMER. It's messed up because I was left living with the woman who basically drove him away.

He was a good dad, what I remember of him anyway… *he* never had a problem with me dressing up, he'd even play Ariel to my Ursula, sometimes.

THE PLAYWRIGHT. You should try and find him, it might help with, you know…

THE PERFORMER. He still left us.

Anyway, Sandra was convinced he'd turn up unannounced and start World War Three, so she moved us to Manchester to be closer to her sister when I was thirteen.

I went off the rails, sneaking off to the gay village to go clubbing… and the rest.

That's where Janelle spotted me.

THE PLAYWRIGHT. Now there's a name you've mentioned a few times before.

THE PERFORMER. Because she felt more like a mum than Sandra ever did.

Saw me dancing on the podium in Essentials, marched straight over and demanded I come to her dance school in Longsight.

If I hadn't met Janelle, I wouldn't have gone down to London to train professionally and I definitely wouldn't have opened my own dance school.

She saw my potential and she pushed me.

Sandra barely got food on the table, too busy killing herself with fags and booze, crying about how much she'd messed up her sad little life.

THE PLAYWRIGHT. They were right when they said, 'your parents fuck you up.'

THE PERFORMER. Yeah, but not yours.

THE PLAYWRIGHT. Babes we had 'the sex conversation' after I'd already had sex and got HIV.

THE PERFORMER. Touché.

A pause.

THE PERFORMER *is staring intently at* THE PLAYWRIGHT *who is slightly oblivious to this attention.*

THE PLAYWRIGHT. Still not been served.

Maybe he *is* just a shit waiter.

THE PERFORMER (*impulsive*). Marry me.

THE PLAYWRIGHT. Sorry, what?

THE PERFORMER. Marry me.

THE PLAYWRIGHT. Are you messing?

THE PERFORMER. No.

I've never been more certain of anything in my life.

Marry me.

For God's sake, we're in our thirties, practically dead on the gay scene.

THE PLAYWRIGHT (*hesitant*). Erm… I don't know.

I really wasn't expecting –

THE PERFORMER. – neither was I but… I've just shared stuff with you I've never shared with anyone.

(*Shouting.*) I've shared my load with you.

THE PLAYWRIGHT. I'm under no impression that I'm the first to receive that.

THE PERFORMER. No, but I was *your* first… since him.

Marry me.

At least we'll get fucking served if you say 'yes'.

THE PLAYWRIGHT. Oh my God this is crazy, you're crazy.

THE PERFORMER. Don't hold it against me.

THE PLAYWRIGHT. Okay.

Let's get married.

THE PERFORMER. Really?

THE PLAYWRIGHT. Yeah, why not?

They embrace excitedly.

THE PERFORMER. Oh my God!

THE PLAYWRIGHT. Oh my God!

THE PERFORMER. Till the world ends.

Moment Ten: Eat, Sleep, Rave, Shag, Repeat

Mid-2018 – early 2019. A blurred mess of house parties, raves and afterparties.

House music plays.

THE PLAYWRIGHT (*on mic*). It's like time sped up after that.

You proposed properly at Pride, down on one knee in front of the crowds, the lot.

And despite knowing it was the exact opposite of what I wanted to say or do.

I just went along with it.

Why the fuck did I just go along with it?

Visuals and club lighting.

They dance.

A drug-fucked blur of parties, drugs, after parties and sex – projected visuals of photos from endless messy nights out fill the space.

But there's a creeping repetition and it's less magical, less romantic than before.

They dance in a club, side by side but not acknowledging one another – totally out of it on drugs.

THE PERFORMER *dances alone as* THE PLAYWRIGHT *moves the stage blocks for the next scene.*

Time to call it a night.

THE PLAYWRIGHT *grabs a coat, and they land at…*

Moment Eleven: Do You Want To Have A Threesome?

Spring 2019. A tram stop in Manchester.

It's early morning and they've just emerged from an all-night queer rave.

The sun is just coming up and we can hear the sounds of the city waking and the birds tweeting.

THE PLAYWRIGHT. It was proper fun tonight; almost as wild as Pride last year after you proposed, remember?

THE PERFORMER. Yeah.

(*Under their breath.*) It's nearly been a year and we've still not set a date.

THE PLAYWRIGHT. Dean's invited us back to his for afters.

THE PERFORMER. I'm not sure I'm feeling it babe.

THE PLAYWRIGHT. Alright Mother T, pipe down.

THE PERFORMER. Maybe if Dean spent some money on therapy instead of drugs, his life wouldn't be such a fuck-up.

THE PLAYWRIGHT. Erm, you can talk.

THE PERFORMER. And what happened to the nun I met on our first date anyway?

Only done a bit of coke, my arse.

You're the biggest hoover of the lot, going to start calling you Henry.

THE PLAYWRIGHT. Okay, so maybe I lied a bit about my past, so shoot me.

I'm not as confident as you on a first date.

Anyway, what's the point in therapy when the whole world has gone to shit?

Might as well just enjoy it whilst it lasts.

A pause.

THE PERFORMER *is cold.*

THE PLAYWRIGHT *takes off his coat and places it over their shoulders.*

They sit watching the sunrise.

Nice sunrise.

THE PERFORMER *pauses, something is weighing heavy.*

THE PERFORMER. Before I met you, I was a mess you know?

Living for the weekend.

It's why I came back up here, fresh start, and now look at us, out every weekend.

THE PLAYWRIGHT. Not every weekend.

THE PERFORMER. Feels like it.

THE PLAYWRIGHT. Then stop!

THE PERFORMER. But I enjoy it… do I enjoy it?

THE PLAYWRIGHT. Yeah, I'm getting mixed messages here.

THE PERFORMER. Some days I think I'm only still here because of pills.

Uppers, downers, disco biscuits, SSRIs, PrEP… a very queer prescription.

You know, when PrEP came along, before you could even get it on the NHS, I bought some online, but then I thought, what's the point?

I've shagged my way around half of London, probably going to get it anyway, aren't I?

Might as well have a brief window where I can enjoy not being kept alive by a pill.

How fucked up is that?

THE PLAYWRIGHT (*pissed off*). Fairly fucked up.

Do you want to have a threesome?

THE PERFORMER. Okay, where did that come from?

THE PLAYWRIGHT. I dunno, you always talk about your life in London, and it seems so exotic and exciting.

THE PERFORMER. I would trade all the threesomes and sex parties in the world to have found you sooner.

THE PLAYWRIGHT. That's sweet, but you know deep down it's not true.

You could put it about in your twenties, I hadn't even had sex without a condom until I met you.

THE PERFORMER. Which is why it's special.

THE PLAYWRIGHT. Oh, so you can happily retire from your fuck-boy fantasy life, but me?

I might as well check-in to the old folks home now.

THE PERFORMER. I was your first time without condoms, that's *our thing*, I don't want to risk ruining that.

THE PLAYWRIGHT. That's a bit possessive.

THE PERFORMER. Why'd you think I put a ring on it?

A pause.

THE PERFORMER. I don't know, maybe you're right.

I can't open up Pandora's box of sexual delights in front of you and then be a cock-blocker when you run free of your harness.

THE PLAYWRIGHT. Erm, I wasn't a nun before we met.

Maybe a bit vanilla.

THE PERFORMER. Babes, you thought HnH meant 'Has No Hair'.

They both burst out laughing.

THE PLAYWRIGHT. Just one threesome.

If we have fun, great, if we don't, at least I got it out of my system.

Another pause as THE PERFORMER *considers the proposition.*

THE PERFORMER. Okay.

But if we have a threesome, you can't be fucked though, deal?

Oh, and they can't be called Keith, I could never sleep with a man called Keith.

There, I said it, I've said my piece, I've shared with the group.

THE PLAYWRIGHT. What about Nigel?

THE PERFORMER. Hmm… on the maybe pile.

THE PLAYWRIGHT. Bruce?

THE PERFORMER. Absolutely not, I draw the line.

THE PLAYWRIGHT. I'd have a Bruce over a Nigel any day, Bruce might be a fit Australian.

Nigel still lives with his mum and wants to show off his collection of dead moths before nutting you.

THE PERFORMER. Ooh, I love dead moths, very early noughties Christina Aguilera.

Come on, it's cold, let's go home, before your jaw knocks someone out.

THE PLAYWRIGHT. Oh my God, am I gurning?

THE PERFORMER *does an over-the-top impression of* THE PLAYWRIGHT *chewing their cheeks*.

THE PLAYWRIGHT. Oh my God, don't!

They both laugh as they exit.

Moment Twelve: Nine Inch Nick

Late spring 2019. The living room of their terraced house.

Music plays with sound effects from the world of online dating mixed in.

The projected visuals delve deep into the world of Grindr and other hook-up apps:

HnH. PnP. BB Only. No fats, no femmes. Masc4masc. R u clean? Gym fit only. No timewasters. No 'theys' only gays. No uglies. Straight acting only. No fuglies, no faceless profiles, no foreigners.

They grab their phones and dance a duet – the phone screens light their faces.

THE PERFORMER *takes to the microphone leaving* THE PLAYWRIGHT *frantically messaging people on his phone.*

THE PERFORMER (*on mic*). It's like time sped up after that.

> After I agreed to the threesome, you were like a kid in a candy shop suggesting guys… all of them white.
>
> And despite knowing that it was the exact opposite of what I wanted to say or do.
>
> I just went along with it.
>
> Why the fuck did I just go along with it?

And snap, we're back in the house.

THE PLAYWRIGHT. Nine Inch Nick.

> Jeez, will you look at him.

THE PERFORMER. He's in his forties.

THE PLAYWRIGHT. And?

> Idris Elba is fifty-one and you always claim he's your free pass.

THE PERFORMER. Okay, fair.

> But don't forget he's not fucking you because that's *our thing*.

THE PLAYWRIGHT (*to himself*). Well aren't you a lucky thing then getting those nine inches all to yourself?

The doorbell goes.

THE PERFORMER. And then before we know it, the night arrives and he's here.

A snap fantasy – unsettling music plays.

THE PERFORMER *welcomes Nick into the lounge and begins to undress.*

THE PLAYWRIGHT *undoes his belt and top button.*

THE PLAYWRIGHT *becomes Nick, takes the mic and holds it from his crotch.*

THE PERFORMER *slowly dances down to their knees, ready to suck, then slowly turns round ready to be fucked.*

THE PLAYWRIGHT *moves down to his knees and thrusts the microphone between* THE PERFORMER*'s legs.*

A sharp intake of breath, THE PERFORMER *enjoys 'taking' Nick's nine inches.*

They writhe slowly, almost grotesque-like.

THE PLAYWRIGHT *passes the microphone through* THE PERFORMER*'s legs from behind and steps back.*

THE PERFORMER *continues to writhe like being fucked whilst 'sucking' the mic.*

THE PLAYWRIGHT *steps out of the scene suddenly and observes, an out of body experience.*

THE PERFORMER *continues to writhe and contort their face – slow-motion sex looks really fucking scary.*

Suddenly the lounge phone rings loudly.

It startles THE PLAYWRIGHT, *but* THE PERFORMER *doesn't appear to be able to hear it.*

THE PLAYWRIGHT *slowly makes his way over to it.*

The cacophony of sound is building, building, building…

We hear voices swirling and echoing:

(Ex-lover) *'Take this, it'll help you relax…downstairs.'*

(Ex-lover's friend) *'It's fine, we take it all the time.'*

(Coach Carr) *'You will get chlamydia and die!'*

(Nurse) 'I'm afraid to say the results came back positive.'

More phones ringing loudly.

Sounds of hard rhythmic fucking.

Someone wincing in pain, not enjoying it.

Hearts beating.

Hard fucking.

Heavy breathing.

Everything rising, up, up and up.

Horror movie-level terrifying.

THE PLAYWRIGHT *is paralysed with fear over the phone, he's hyperventilating.*

He stares at the phone in terror.

A huge rush as he picks up the phone and puts it to his ear.

Everything stops, the phone goes dead, a three-pitch dial tone.

Whoosh: and we're back.

(As though nothing has happened.) You okay, babe?

THE PLAYWRIGHT. Yeah.

THE PERFORMER. Why you holding the phone?

THE PLAYWRIGHT. I don't know, must've rung again.

Maybe we should get rid of it.

He places it back on the receiver as THE PERFORMER *places the microphone back on its stand.*

Has Nick gone?

THE PERFORMER. Yeah, just now.

THE PLAYWRIGHT. He was proper fit.

THE PERFORMER. So fit.

But he's not you.

Fancy a cuddle upstairs, just me and you this time?

THE PLAYWRIGHT. Erm, yeah, sure.

Just let me get a glass of water first.

THE PERFORMER *exits*.

THE PLAYWRIGHT *is still fixated on the phone, terrified it might ring again.*

But this time there's nothing.

Silence.

Deafening silence.

He checks to make sure THE PERFORMER *has gone upstairs, then takes the receiver off the hook.*

He collects his things, takes one last look at the room, then leaves.

Moment Thirteen: Phone Fight

Summer 2019. The living room of their terraced house.

THE PLAYWRIGHT *is sat on his phone*.

THE PERFORMER *comes in from work, flustered from a stressful day.*

The air is heavy with unresolved tension, conversations that have yet to be spoken.

THE PLAYWRIGHT. You're late.

Been texting you.

THE PERFORMER. Sorry, class ran over a bit; you know what it's like before the big summer showcase.

And that kid's parent, you know the one I was telling you about, I swear she uses the wrong pronouns on purpose.

Fucking Karen.

THE PLAYWRIGHT. Not everyone is up to speed on pronouns, babe.

THE PERFORMER. Why do you never have my back?

THE PLAYWRIGHT. Sometimes it feels like you're just looking for it.

THE PERFORMER. For what?

THE PLAYWRIGHT. A reason to be pissed off with the world.

THE PERFORMER. Don't you think my rage is justified?

THE PLAYWRIGHT. Do you remember that time when we were first dating?

In the pizza shop?

When that guy called you the n-word and I laid into him, remember?

And afterwards you said, 'I don't need you to fight my battles for me, babes.'

I was devastated I got it so wrong, so, now I let you fight on your own.

THE PERFORMER. Have you been on the sofa all day?

THE PLAYWRIGHT *returns to his phone, texting.*

THE PLAYWRIGHT. No, I've been writing.

THE PERFORMER. I'm not being funny, but writing isn't paying the bills.

(*Under their breath.*) And it definitely won't pay for our wedding, whenever the hell that's going to be.

THE PLAYWRIGHT. Please don't start –

THE PERFORMER. It's Pride next week.

A whole year since I proposed and you said 'yes', except you've not really committed to anything, have you?

When *can* you fit me in around your *ever* so busy writing schedule?

THE PLAYWRIGHT. It's a big decision; look I'm not getting dragged in to another argument with you about it.

THE PERFORMER. Will you get off your phone when I'm speaking to you, for God's sake?

THE PLAYWRIGHT *pointedly puts his phone down and gives his full attention to* THE PERFORMER.

What exactly are you doing on there anyway?

You're never off the damn thing.

THE PLAYWRIGHT. I'm texting my friend.

(*Under his breath*.) Bloody paranoid.

THE PERFORMER. Yeah, not without good reason.

THE PLAYWRIGHT. Not this *again*.

I was messaging a guy about hooking up with *both* of us because let's face it, bringing in another guy is the only way to get any sexual kicks round here anymore.

THE PERFORMER. *You* asked to open up this relationship.

THE PLAYWRIGHT. Yeah, but you didn't take much convincing though, did you?

And you know, despite the amount of dick you've been enjoying, I've still kept the promise you asked of me.

Our thing is still *our thing*.

THE PLAYWRIGHT *goes to leave*.

THE PERFORMER. Prove it.

Show me your phone.

THE PLAYWRIGHT. Are you messing?

> THE PERFORMER *tries to grab the phone as* THE PLAYWRIGHT *passes.*

What the hell are you doing?

THE PERFORMER. Give me your phone.

> I've been cheated on enough to know when someone's lying to me.

Give me the fucking phone!

> THE PERFORMER *lunges for the phone and manages to grab it but* THE PLAYWRIGHT *still has hold of it too.*
>
> *They tussle a bit, gently at first, but then it escalates.*
>
> THE PERFORMER *shoves* THE PLAYWRIGHT *who stumbles backwards onto the sofa, in the scuffle* THE PLAYWRIGHT *loses his grip on the phone.*
>
> *A pause.*
>
> THE PLAYWRIGHT *lunges at* THE PERFORMER *pushing them up against a wall trying to get the phone back.*
>
> *They stare each other down.*
>
> THE PERFORMER *leans in as though they are going to kiss* THE PLAYWRIGHT, *but* THE PLAYWRIGHT *pulls away.*
>
> *Silence.*

THE PLAYWRIGHT. Password is blancheanddorothy4eva – all lower case.

> *In a fit of rage,* THE PERFORMER *launches the phone out of the front door, and it clatters on the hard concrete outside.*

Have you lost the plot?!

I'm calling the police.

THE PERFORMER. You wouldn't fucking dare.

> THE PLAYWRIGHT *runs to the landline phone,* THE PERFORMER *follows quickly.*

Another fight, a proper fight this time.

THE PERFORMER *grabs the phone receiver accidentally hitting* THE PLAYWRIGHT *on the chin with it in the process.*

THE PLAYWRIGHT *sees red and retaliates hitting* THE PERFORMER *across the face with the receiver.*

They both stop, horrified at what they're doing.

THE PERFORMER *is bleeding from their mouth.*

THE PLAYWRIGHT *is nursing his chin.*

They are both stunned by what has just happened.

High pitched ringing.

(*Close to tears.*) After everything I told you.

Suddenly there's a loud banging at the front door: Lakeisha.

THE PLAYWRIGHT *gestures with his head to* THE PERFORMER*: you're going to need to answer that.*

But THE PERFORMER *is frozen to the spot with fear.*

Eventually THE PERFORMER *goes to the door.*

LAKEISHA (*voice-over*). Hiya, everything alright?

Just heard a bit of –

THE PERFORMER (*masking tears*). Yeah everything's fine Lakeisha.

We were just getting some stuff out the attic, dropped a suitcase down the stairs.

LAKEISHA (*voice-over*). Darnell was putting the bins out and found this phone in the alley.

Not yours, is it?

THE PERFORMER. I'm not sure, they all look the same these days, don't they?

Anyway, I've got to go Lakeisha, he's stuck up in the attic without a ladder to get back down.

Achingly beautiful music plays.

THE PLAYWRIGHT *leaves.*

THE PERFORMER *sits and cries deep, uncontrollable, guttural sobs.*

Moment Fourteen: A (Very) Toxic Gig

Autumn 2019. The lounge of their terraced house and the Manchester Arena.

THE PERFORMER *is sat on the sofa.*

THE PLAYWRIGHT *enters and puts on a jacket as though going to leave.*

He pulls an envelope out of his pocket, hesitates, then...

THE PLAYWRIGHT. I got you an early Christmas present.

   THE PERFORMER *opens the envelope.*

THE PERFORMER. Tickets to see Britney Spears, are you kidding me, these must have cost a fortune.

THE PLAYWRIGHT. I wanted to say sorry, for what happened, we've not really spoken about it much.

THE PERFORMER. Small talk keeps us safe, right?

THE PLAYWRIGHT. You spoken to the doctor yet?

THE PERFORMER. They'll just fob me off with some sertraline and tell me to download a mindfulness app.

   (*Sarcastic.*) World beating National Health Service.

   You should be getting help too –

THE PLAYWRIGHT. – I know.

   I'm not the enemy here, I just…

THE PERFORMER. Sorry.

Britney will be amazing.

Thank you.

THE PERFORMER *kisses him on the cheek.*

A flourish of activity as we move to the arena.

They take off their jackets to reveal iconic Britney Spears costumes. THE PERFORMER *is dressed as sexy air hostess Britney and* THE PLAYWRIGHT *as sexy schoolgirl Britney.*

THE PLAYWRIGHT. The build up to the Britney gig was… intense.

THE PERFORMER. But I'd cut back on the drinking.

THE PLAYWRIGHT. And the dealer was sending me promotional offers it had been that long.

THE PERFORMER. So, we arrive at the arena and it's a typical Mancunian autumn night.

A crack of thunder and the sound of rain.

We're stood outside in the bag check queue which always takes ages since the bomb.

THE PLAYWRIGHT. And I'm in front and get waved through but once I'm inside I turn around and they're nowhere to be seen.

THE PERFORMER. Because, quelle surprise, I've been profiled for drugs.

THE PLAYWRIGHT. I'm sure they didn't single you out because you're –

THE PERFORMER. – really?

This is the hill you're choosing to die on.

THE PLAYWRIGHT. Why do you have to ruin everything nice we do?

Yes, racism exists, yes, it's fucking shit and I hate you have to deal with it.

But on this occasion, you're seeing something that didn't happen... you're wearing a bag for Christ's sake!

They check everyone with bags!

And even if it was them being racist, sometimes for your own sanity you have just got to rise above it.

THE PERFORMER *storms off*.

(*To the audience*.) So, we're off to a good start.

Anyway, I go to find the seats and hope that they cool off and come and join me.

THE PERFORMER *returns*.

And they do ten minutes later – carrying four pints.

THE PERFORMER. What!?

The queue's massive, we don't want to miss the gig.

THE PLAYWRIGHT. We agreed one pint.

THE PERFORMER (*cutting*). Just call it a peace offering.

THE PLAYWRIGHT. So, we sit in silence drinking our pints like *that* fucking couple as everyone else in the arena buzzes with excitement.

THE PERFORMER. And we've nearly finished both pints already, so he breaks the silence and says:

THE PLAYWRIGHT. I'll get some more before it starts.

THE PERFORMER. Get four more.

THE PLAYWRIGHT (*pointedly*). I'll get two.

>THE PLAYWRIGHT *turns to the back and stands waiting at the bar.*

>THE PERFORMER *looks around checking the coast is clear, then sniffs a discreet key of coke.*

>THE PLAYWRIGHT *turns back around, returning from the bar catching them in the act.*

>THE PERFORMER *freezes*.

THE PERFORMER (*trying to break the tension*). Oh well, Christmas soon, innit?

THE PLAYWRIGHT. Clearly the drugs search you kicked off about wasn't very thorough, was it?

We hear an unmistakable riff of Ms Spears over cheering crowds.

A snap fantasy – they briefly become Britney as they grab the microphones and bring them downstage.

THE PERFORMER (*on mic*). And then Britney is right there.

But we're both too wound up to really care.

THE PLAYWRIGHT (*on mic*). And a few songs in all that pre-show beer is pressing on my bladder.

THE PLAYWRIGHT *turns to the back and mimes having a piss in a urinal.*

THE PERFORMER. So, he goes to the toilet, and he takes far too long, there's no way he's just having a piss.

THE PLAYWRIGHT (*turning and shouting from the 'toilet'*). I'd had three pints; it was just a really long wee.

THE PERFORMER. Yeah, a really long wee that involved a bag and a key.

THE PLAYWRIGHT *turns back to the front trying to cover up he's just sniffed drugs in the toilet.*

THE PLAYWRIGHT. And then time sort of sped up after that.

The sounds of the gig speed up – faster, faster.

THE PERFORMER. Suddenly there's another pint.

A whoosh as they spin around 360 degrees.

THE PLAYWRIGHT. And another pint.

They spin around 360 degrees again.

THE PERFORMER. And another.

They spin around 360 degrees again.

THE PLAYWRIGHT. A key in the toilets.

They both sniff as they spin again.

THE PERFORMER. A pill from some random stranger.

They spin again.

THE PLAYWRIGHT. And then one right in front of everyone in the arena.

They both sniff as they spin again – they're now totally fucked.

They both stand there sort of half dancing.

(*Slurring.*) And then one of us spills a pint all over the girl in front.

THE PERFORMER. And she says:

THE PLAYWRIGHT (*as the beer-soaked girl*). Ah nah, what the fuck are yous playing at!?

And they say:

THE PERFORMER. Oh my god, we are so sorry, babes.

We'll get you a drink to make up for it.

THE PLAYWRIGHT. But we've chosen the wrong girl to spill our drink over and her and her mate turn on us shouting over the music.

THE PERFORMER. And he says:

THE PLAYWRIGHT. Leave it, babes, rise above it.

And they say:

THE PERFORMER. You must be fucking kidding me!

And then she says:

THE PLAYWRIGHT (*as the beer-soaked girl*). What are the stupid pair of faggots wearing anyway?'

And then they say:

THE PERFORMER. It's faggots like us that put Britney where she is.

THE PLAYWRIGHT. And they throw another pint straight in her face and storm off.

THE PERFORMER *exits*.

And I'm left standing there.

The remaining half of *that* fucking couple.

And then Britney hits the chorus of 'Till the World Ends'.

The music rises up and up and up and up and up.

THE PLAYWRIGHT *faces straight ahead, fighting back tears as the arena goes wild around them.*

The last four lines of 'Till the World Ends' plays.

Bass drop.

The crowd cheers in the distance

THE PLAYWRIGHT *exits*.

Moment Fifteen: Spit In My Face, Part 2

Immediately following. Outside the Manchester Arena.

THE PLAYWRIGHT *approaches*.

THE PLAYWRIGHT. Well, what a waste of money that was.

THE PERFORMER. That homophobic bitch deserved it.

Don't –

THE PLAYWRIGHT. Don't what?

THE PERFORMER. Don't tell me I should have risen above it.

You never have my back.

THE PLAYWRIGHT. Not when you act like that, you're an embarrassment.

THE PERFORMER. You know when I fell in love with you, I actually fell in love with my mother.

THE PLAYWRIGHT. It's such a cop out to blame her for your own shitty behaviour.

THE PERFORMER. Oh, believe me, I wish I didn't have to.

You threatened to call the police on me... after everything I'd told you.

THE PLAYWRIGHT. You'd gone feral, I didn't know what else to do.

THE PERFORMER. Oh, I'll show you feral.

THE PERFORMER *gets out their phone and scrolls to find a number.*

THE PLAYWRIGHT. What are you doing?

THE PERFORMER (*on the phone*). Oh hi Diane, how are you...

No everything is fine, sorry it's late...

I'm with him now, yeah, we've just come out the gig... yeah it was great...

No, everything is fine honestly, he's just got something he wants to tell you.

THE PERFORMER *holds out the phone to* THE PLAYWRIGHT *who is frozen to the spot.*

(*On the phone.*) He seems a little tongue-tied Diane.

It's understandable when you've been lying to your mum about being HIV+ for most of your life.

THE PLAYWRIGHT. You wouldn't dare.

THE PERFORMER (*putting the phone away*). Maybe not, but now we're even.

THE PLAYWRIGHT. You're a piece of work, you know that?

THE PERFORMER. Takes one to know one.

THE PLAYWRIGHT. No, I'm not getting sucked into it this time.

You're messed up.

Making me abstain whilst you get fucked in front of me?

And yeah, I know I was the one who asked for a threesome, because that's what we do, don't we?

Greedy fucking gays, we have to ruin every nice thing we ever get in this life.

You know, maybe I have been getting fucked.

Nine Inch Nick came round again and did me over the kitchen counter, except he didn't because if you'd been paying attention, you'd know I hate having sex.

Every time someone comes near me it all comes –

After all the years of shit and shame and slurs I thought, finally, I can be free, I thought undetectable meant I'm not toxic anymore... but you... you make me feel like I still am.

THE PERFORMER. You want to try walking in these shoes babes, you wouldn't last a minute.

(*A gut-wrenching realisation.*) She only shagged him because she fancied a bit of – [Black cock].

(*Through tears.*) The biggest whoopsie of the lot.

I genuinely thought you were the one who finally got it.

THE PLAYWRIGHT (*fighting back tears*). I do get it.

I do.

THE PERFORMER. You have broken my heart, and I wish I'd never met you.

THE PERFORMER *goes to leave*.

THE PLAYWRIGHT. And now you just walk away... must run in the family.

THE PERFORMER *turns on their heels and spits in* THE PLAYWRIGHT'*s face.*

They stare at one another for what feels like an eternity.

Give me the keys –

THE PERFORMER. I'm sorry I didn't –

THE PLAYWRIGHT. – the keys, NOW.

GIVE ME THE FUCKING KEYS.

THE PERFORMER *gives* THE PLAYWRIGHT *the house keys.*

THE PERFORMER (*a pathetic attempt at humour*). You used to like it.

THE PLAYWRIGHT. Yeah, where's Lakeisha when you really need her, hey?

THE PERFORMER (*sudden desperation*). Please don't leave me.

THE PLAYWRIGHT. Look at us, arguing in the street, we are broken.

THE PERFORMER. We can fix it.

We can fix our thing, we can fix everything, you and me, together, to the end of eternity.

Remember?

We can fix us.

THE PLAYWRIGHT. I'm not so sure we can.

THE PLAYWRIGHT *leaves.*

Music rushes up.

Moment Sixteen: The Message Does Not Get Through

Immediately following. A journey between the arena and their terraced house.

Fractured drum and bass music, a buzzing like when you're too high, and the sound of rain and cars whizzing by.

THE PERFORMER *appears on the street in the rain.*

They take out their phone and dial waiting frantically for THE PLAYWRIGHT *to pick up.*

No answer.

THE PERFORMER *is spiralling.*

They take a sniff of drugs and then try and call THE PLAYWRIGHT *again.*

THE PLAYWRIGHT *appears on the street in the rain.*

He looks at his phone, hangs up and puts it away.

He takes a sniff of drugs.

THE PERFORMER *begins running, anywhere, who cares anymore.*

THE PLAYWRIGHT *vomits and then begins running in the other direction.*

Music, sound effects, projections and lights collude to make this one hell of a bad trip.

The cold sting of the night air, people puking in the gutter, arguments and shouting, beeping horns, blurred text messages, phones ringing, dial tones, voicemail messages:

'*You have twenty-two new voice messages. Message one. Message deleted. Message two. Message deleted. Message three. Message deleted. Message four. Message deleted. Message five. Message deleted.*'

They stop, look at each other, scream and tear the house straight in two with an almighty cracking and fracturing.

Make it stop, please make it stop, just make it all stop.

Moment Seventeen: Here Comes the Bit Where It Hurts (Or, How You [I] Nearly Died)

Immediately following. Outside and inside their terraced house.

Sounds echo from the previous scene, the visuals swirl and pulse.

THE PLAYWRIGHT *runs through the front door and slams it shut, slumping to the floor in the hallway.*

Shaking, he pulls out a bag of gear and does a couple of keys.

THE PERFORMER *appears at the door: bang, bang, bang, bang!*

THE PERFORMER. Let me in I need a piss!

No reply.

Bang, bang, bang, bang, bang!

You've got my keys, let me in!

I'm sorry, I don't know what came over me.

I need a piss, let me in!

Bang, bang, bang, bang, bang!

A rush of something uncontrollable, THE PERFORMER *decides the only way is to punch through the window: smash!*

Everything fractures and smashes into pieces.

A cacophony of sounds.

Fuck!

THE PLAYWRIGHT (*screaming*). Stay away from me you fucking nutcase!

THE PERFORMER (*shouting*). I'm bleeding, fuck!

Help me I've cut myself I'm bleeding! Shit! Fuck!

Call me an ambulance I've cut my hand open! Please help me!

Open the door I'm bleeding!

THE PLAYWRIGHT *looks down at their hand… it's also covered in blood.*

He's drunk, drug fucked and spinning out.

Voices and sounds from the world of the play echo, distort, flicker and splutter.

A dark, unsettling and swirling version of 'Toxic' by Britney Spears begins.

THE PLAYWRIGHT. Too high, can't come down.

THE PLAYWRIGHT *continues to perform lines from 'Toxic' by Britney Spears.*

THE PERFORMER *appears stage right climbing round the flat of the set onto a ledge, teetering.*

They slowly make their way in front of the window, clinging on and trying to get into the house.

THE PLAYWRIGHT *turns to see* THE PERFORMER *teetering on the edge of the precipice.*

He clambers up the other side of the set trying to reach them.

The music is rising, rising, rising – unbearable.

They reach out for one another.

A haunting whisper: here comes the bit where it hurts!

A humongous climax.

They both fall to the floor.

Blackout.

Then silence.

White noise, fading, flickering.

Eventually the darkness is broken with a small amount of light.

THE PLAYWRIGHT *breathes an almighty intake of breath and sits up.*

He sees THE PERFORMER *on the floor and scrabbles for the mic to try and tell the rest of the story.*

THE PLAYWRIGHT. And then I run outside.

And Lakeisha's there in her dressing gown.

And I look down and you're on the floor.

Bleeding.

And I can't breathe.

LAKEISHA (*voice-over*). 'Darnell, call an ambulance.

It's next door, they've fallen off the bloody drainpipe trying to get in the house.'

Sirens can be heard in the distance.

A faint blue flashing light.

I can't breathe.

I can't breathe.

Help me breathe.

Please breathe.

Please breathe.

Faint medical beeping.

Everything flatlines.

Moment Eighteen: An Epilogue (Of Sorts)

The present moment.

The lights slowly come up.

THE PLAYWRIGHT. So, that was the story of how we met, fell in love and fucked it up.

THE PERFORMER. But it's not just our story.

THE PLAYWRIGHT. It's his, and his… and theirs.

THE PERFORMER. Maybe it was yours.

Maybe.

THE PLAYWRIGHT. Most of what you've seen tonight *was* true.

THE PERFORMER. Every pill popped, every face snogged, every line snorted, every cock sucked, every slur shouted, every fist raised happened… to someone.

THE PLAYWRIGHT. You know it was me who fell out of the window, right?

THE PERFORMER. It doesn't really matter who said this or who did that.

THE PLAYWRIGHT. No.

I just really wish I could say sorry.

How fucked up is that?

THE PERFORMER. Fairly fucked up.

But it's your play, so you can play out any damn fantasy you please.

Moment Nineteen: Phone Fantasy (Or, I Think I'm Ready Now)

An imagined time and place.

They take the microphones set them up like the opening of the show.

Music plays, a soulful house beat with a gentle phone ringing.

THE PLAYWRIGHT (*on mic*). They told us it was a gift.

To be like us

Every day

They say

Be full of pride

To show the world

That shame won't break you.

THE PERFORMER. But sometimes it does.

I'm not proud of everything in my life, are you?

THE PLAYWRIGHT. No, I've hurt a lot of people.

I hurt you.

THE PERFORMER. Hurt people, hurt people.

THE PLAYWRIGHT. And so, the cycle continues.

THE PERFORMER. Does it though?

THE PLAYWRIGHT. We went through a lot, didn't we?

THE PERFORMER. Yeah, we did.

THE PLAYWRIGHT. I'm sorry.

THE PERFORMER. We did the best we could with what we had at the time.

And just look at Britney.

She survived 2007, and a whole lot more.

THE PLAYWRIGHT. I really hope you're okay now, wherever you are, whatever you're doing.

THE PERFORMER. Yeah, same.

THE PLAYWRIGHT. Oh, I got that therapy like you always said I should.

THE PERFORMER. And I found my dad.

THE PLAYWRIGHT. Really?

THE PERFORMER. We've not met yet... early days.

But it's a start.

THE PLAYWRIGHT. I guess.

I'm not going to say I love you, because I don't, maybe I did, once upon time.

THE PERFORMER. Yeah.

I am proud though, of who we're becoming.

THE PLAYWRIGHT. Me too.

It was a laugh at times, wasn't it?

THE PERFORMER. Yeah... intoxicating.

And I know what you're going to say, 'intoxicating can so easily become toxic.'

THE PLAYWRIGHT. Maybe you do know me better than I thought.

(*Singing*.) 'Intoxicate me now, with your lovin' now.'

THE PERFORMER (*singing*). I think I'm ready now.

THE PLAYWRIGHT (*spoken*). I think I'm ready now.

THE PLAYWRIGHT *turns to look at the performer.*

The music swells.

They hold hands and get ready to face the world together one more time.

Maybe this time around.

Maybe.

Just maybe.

A deep intake of breath.

THE PLAYWRIGHT. This is the story of how we met, fell in love and –

A final swoosh, like a candle being snuffed out.

Blackout.

A Glossary

HIV (Human Immunodeficiency Virus)
A virus that attacks the immune system, present in bodily fluids. Transmitted though unprotected sexual contact, blood to blood (e.g. sharing needles) and mother to baby during birth/ breastfeeding (this last way is rare thanks to screening and medication).

Advanced HIV
A less stigmatised term now often used in place of AIDS.

PrEP (Pre-Exposure Prophylaxis)
Medication taken before sex to prevent transmission of HIV. Highly effective if taken as prescribed. Available on the NHS in England, Scotland and Wales. Condoms remain an effective method of preventing HIV transmission.

U=U (Undetectable=Untransmittable)
A person who has been on HIV treatment for over six months, whose viral load is 'undetectable', cannot pass the virus on to others.

SSRIs
A type of anti-depressant medication commonly prescribed in the UK.

For up-to-date information on HIV always seek advice from reputable websites.

We recommend:
www.tht.org.uk | www.ght.org.uk | www.nat.org.uk | www.unaids.org

Dibby Theatre

Dibby Theatre is an award-winning LGBTQ+ national touring theatre company led by Artistic Director Nathaniel J Hall and Producer Ross Carey. Their mission is simple; to strive for a world where all LGBTQ+ people can live authentically and with pride.

www.dibbytheatre.org
@DibbyTheatre

HOME

HOME is Manchester's centre for international contemporary culture. HOME works with international and UK artists to produce extraordinary theatrical experiences, producing an exciting mix of thought-provoking drama, dance and festivals, with a strong focus on international work, new commissions and talent development.

www.homemcr.org
@HOME_mcr

www.nickhernbooks.co.uk

@nickhernbooks